MW01232987

Our Father, Hallowed be thy Name

Neil C. Ellis

WORD & SPIRIT
PUBLISHING

Our Father, Hallowed be thy Name
© 2020 by Neil C. Ellis
ISBN: 978-1-949106-43-5

Published by Word and Spirit Publishing
P.O. Box 701403
Tulsa, Oklahoma 74170
wordandspiritpublishing.com

Contents

Introduction

WHEN GOD, THROUGH JESUS, WALKED ON this earth with His disciples, the disciples thoroughly scrutinized Him. They paid very close attention to His daily routine.

During His three years of ministry, He spent quality time with His disciples. He didn't always have formal instruction times, yet somehow the twelve were always in a classroom, so to speak. Just hanging out with Jesus was a lesson in itself. Consequently, they watched Him. They studied Him. They analyzed Him, and after a while, they recognized a particular pattern. They saw Him healing the sick. They saw Him walking on water. They saw Him restoring hearing to deaf ears. They saw Him at work, and they noticed very carefully that prior to His public ministry times, there was something that was consistently a priority in His life. They saw Him in action, and they were oftentimes present when He performed miracles. However, there's nowhere in scripture where the disciples asked Jesus to teach them how to perform miracles. They never asked Him to teach them how to walk on water. There is no record of them asking Him, "Lord, teach us how to preach." But after analyzing His lifestyle and paying close attention to His daily routine, they recognized something in His life that was not flamboyant, was not public, and as a matter of fact, was only obvious to them during their private times with Him. They noticed that He had a secret weapon: **prayer.**

> *And it came to pass, that, as he was praying in a certain place, when he ceased, one of his disciples said unto him, Lord, teach us to pray.*
>
> —LUKE 11:1

Notice that one of His disciples—most likely, Peter, who was the volunteer spokesman for the disciples—said, "Lord, teach us to pray." They had just finished observing Him in prayer. They watched Him, and what the spokesman was saying, in essence, was:

> *"Lord, we have watched You. We have paid close attention to You. And it's obvious to us where Your power is coming from. We see the miracles You do. We see the powerful connection You have with God, and we want in on that. We've noticed that just prior to You performing any miraculous act, You always spend time in prayer. Lord, teach us to do that. Teach us how to discipline ourselves to pray the way You do."*

It is essential for every believer to have faith and confidence in the power of prayer. We can become so mesmerized by the miraculous that we miss the supernatural. Prayer is the essential foundation upon which every miracle is based. Having faith in prayer is really just having faith in God. We have faith that there is Someone to Whom we are talking. Someone Who loves us, is listening to us, and will fight for us. Unfortunately, so many of us miss it when we don't see immediate results. Our faith wavers because we begin to experience symptoms of an undesirable situation. We can feel pain or sickness in our body which is conflicting with what we are believing for. We may get a notice from the creditor advising that they are going to seize our assets. We may see a post on social media of a cherished child who seems to be further away from God than ever. Situations like this happen every day, and it takes faith to look past what our five senses are telling us and dare to trust in God to see us through.

Notwithstanding our present circumstances, we have to believe that God hears us even when we don't experience some kind of immediate breakthrough. However, we must be convinced that when we pray, God goes to work in our lives, and at the right time, we will see change. So then, where do we begin? What structure should our prayers take? What did Jesus have to say to the disciples when they asked Him to teach them how to pray? These questions and so much more will be addressed as we learn, just as the disciples did, to pray as Jesus prayed.

The Model Prayer

THERE ARE A FEW THINGS IN CHRISTENDOM that are universally accepted. This prayer that the Lord taught His disciples is one of those things. Literally, every denomination, despite its doctrine, despite its beliefs, despite its creeds, use this prayer found in Luke 11.

> *And it came to pass, that, as he was praying in a certain place, when he ceased, one of his disciples said unto him, Lord, teach us to pray, as John also taught his disciples.*
>
> *And he said unto them, When ye pray, say, Our Father which art in heaven, Hallowed be thy name. Thy kingdom come. Thy will be done, as in heaven, so in earth. Give us day by day our daily bread. And forgive us our sins; for we also forgive every one that is indebted to us. And lead us not*

into temptation; but deliver us from evil.

—LUKE 11:1–4

Many people have come to know this prayer as *the Lord's Prayer*. However, calling this prayer the Lord's Prayer is a traditional misnomer. It has been mislabeled by tradition. A more accurate title would be something along the lines of: *The Model Prayer,* or *The Disciples' Prayer,* or even *The Example of Prayer.* The issue I have with calling this prayer the *Lord's Prayer* is the implication that it leaves. The title suggests that Jesus prayed this prayer to the Father in sincerity with regard to His own situation. This simply cannot be, as we can see in Luke 11:4:

…And forgive us our sins; for we also forgive every one that is indebted to us…

Jesus had no sin for which to repent, so Jesus didn't have a reason to pray this prayer in its entirety, which means there must be another reason that He was praying in this manner. Look at Luke 11:2:

And he said unto them, When ye pray, say...

In other words, Jesus was telling us, "When we pray, use this formula. Take this structure that I am giving you and formulate your own prayer to match it." This is not a prayer that should be repeated word for word. It is a framework and a guide for prayer. There is so much more to prayer than a formula or saying the right magic words. That is not the implication here. In fact, I believe the disciples recognized the powerful relationship that Jesus had with the heavenly Father, and they began to desire what Jesus had come to the earth to give them: the opportunity to commune with the Father on a personal and relational level as His sons and daughters. So, what Jesus was teaching them through this prayer is how God the Father prefers to communicate. It's prayer etiquette, or simply put: an outline. And within the framework of this outline, there are headings. With all this in mind, let's examine this prayer from that perspective.

> *Our Father... (Heading Number 1)*
> *Fill in all applicable information for this heading here.

> *Who art in heaven... (Heading Number 2)*
> *Fill in all applicable information for this heading here.

> And so on...

This prayer was never meant to be prayed line for line. The headings provide the structure in the outline to give us a formula for how we ought to shape our prayers; so when we say, "Our Father, Who art in heaven, hallowed be Thy name," we are uttering a list of headings. But based on our knowledge of the scripture, based on our relationship with God, based on our individual situation, and based upon our particular need at the time, we can determine how to fill in the gap after every heading. Discussing outlines, headings, and even the subject of prayer can seem informational but not very exciting, or even something to be desired. Here is the beauty in it, though. The reason that Jesus gave us an outline for prayer instead of a list of words to recite is because doing so would have removed all opportunity for sincerity. You would be praying a formula to receive a desired outcome, instead of talking with your dear Father about a solution that you both want to achieve. To top it all off, Jesus gave us the Holy Spirit to help us, even when we don't know which heading our messed-up situation falls under. Prayer is a wonderful thing. It's not something you get "better at"; it's something you grow in. The more we learn about it, the closer we become to the Father. It is easy to discern the difference between an informed prayer and an uninformed prayer. But we will never be able to tell the difference between a good prayer and a bad prayer. This is because ultimately, prayer comes from the heart (our spirit) and is expressed in faith (our words), through the Author of our faith (Jesus), to our heavenly Father (God), Who then in turn grants our request through the Finisher of our faith (Jesus), and we receive the manifestation of our request by faith (thanksgiving). God has granted all of us a measure of faith, and that faith's strength is incumbent upon our belief in, and mediation on, the Word of God. This prayer is essential to do just that. It helps us keep our lives in God's hands. It helps us organize our thoughts and our feelings and bring them before God with His Word. As an outline, this model prayer can be expanded or condensed as much or as little as we so desire. In other words, this model can be used for a three-to-five-minute prayer, or it can be used for a ten-to-fifteen-minute prayer. And the same model can be used for a thirty-minute prayer, a forty-five-minute prayer, or a fifty-minute prayer, and it's the same model that those of us who know about tarrying before God use. The same model can be used for an hour prayer, a two-hour prayer, or a three-hour prayer.

For however long you decide to pray or feel led to pray, when you follow this model, you will cover every area of your life.

Between the moment when you said "our Father" and the moment when you said "amen," there will not be any need or any issue in your life that you would not have touched.

The structure in this prayer model has a flow to it, and in order to achieve the desired results, you have to go with that flow. The headings in the outline are divided into three major categories. Category number one is all about God:

- Our *Father*
- Who art in heaven
- Hallowed be *Thy* name
- *Thy* kingdom come
- *Thy* will be done.

Now, category two is all about us:

- Give *us* this day *our* daily bread.
- Lead *us* not into temptation.
- Deliver *us* from evil.

And then category three refocuses us back on God:

For *Thine* is the kingdom, the power, and the glory forever and ever. Amen.

So, it begins with God and it ends with God. Some theologians regard this as a "sandwich structure", God at the two ends, with us in the middle. You should not begin your prayers with you, because you're not praying to yourself. Similarly, you should not end your prayers with yourself, because you do not have the power to cause the prayer to come to fruition. That's God's territory.

Our Father

MANY PEOPLE CAN QUOTE THE PRAYER found in the beginning of Luke 11. Even non-Christians could probably get pretty close to reciting it word for word. But the verses following this prayer are a little less known, and they are often separated from the model prayer. In these verses, Jesus frames and reinforces the perspective we should have in regard to prayer. He gives His disciples a model that they can use to pray, and then He begins to feed their faith on the person of God. Read carefully what Jesus says:

> *And he said unto them, Which of you shall have a friend, and shall go unto him at midnight, and say unto him, Friend, lend me three loaves; for a friend of mine in his journey is come to me, and I have nothing to set before him? And he from within shall answer and say,*

Trouble me not: the door is now shut, and my children are with me in bed; I cannot rise and give thee. I say unto you, Though he will not rise and give him, because he is his friend, yet because of his importunity he will rise and give him as many as he needeth. And I say unto you, Ask, and it shall be given you; seek, and ye shall find; knock, and it shall be opened unto you. For every one that asketh receiveth; and he that seeketh findeth; and to him that knocketh it shall be opened. If a son shall ask bread of any of you that is a father, will he give him a stone? or if he ask a fish, will he for a fish give him a serpent? Or if he shall ask an egg, will he offer him a scorpion? If ye then, being evil, know how to give good gifts unto your children: how much more shall your heavenly Father give the Holy Spirit to them that ask him?

LUKE 11:5-13

Jesus revealed three major foundational truths about prayer here. The first is: *God is pleased with faith-filled persistence.*

It takes faith to be persistent. When you and your family are hungry and tired, and you go and knock on God's door, are you willing to stay on God's doorstep until He gives you what you are there for? It's interesting what Jesus calls the person knocking. He calls him "a friend." The designation of "friend" implies that the person knocking knew the master of the household. More than that, he knew what kind of man the master was. He knew what pleased the master. He knew that if he stayed on the doorstep and continued to knock, even if their relationship was not strong enough for the master to invite him in and tell him to take whatever he needed, the master would at least admire his persistence and unfailing faith in the character of the master and grant his request. It will always take faith. Another verse brings more light to this truth:

> *But without faith it is impossible to please him: for he that cometh to God must believe that he is, and that he is a rewarder of them that diligently seek him.*
>
> —HEBREWS 11:6

The second truth is this: God knows what you have need of.

> *...Your Father knows the things you have need of before you ask Him.*
>
> —MATTHEW 6:8 NKJV

Jesus makes the point here that God knows our needs, and He drives the point even further by emphasizing that God knows our needs even before we ask for them. Watch this, then: prayer is not designed to be an informational session in which we inform God of anything. He knows our request before we ask. What God wants to know is whether or not we want to talk to Him about it. But here's the other key—just because God knows about it, does not mean He's going to act on what He knows. He knows everything, but some things He will not act on until there is relational communication with Him that has a key ingredient in it: faith. Many times, people have no real relationship with God. They treat him like a genie in a bottle. They just want to rub a lamp when they have a problem. God then poofs out, grants them whatever they want, and they get to resume life as normal. God did not send Jesus to die on the cross only to save us from hell; He sent Him so that He could adopt us into His family and spend eternity with us.

God is saying:

"I know what you need, but I want to see if you want Me or just want the meeting of your need. Did you come to Me as a last resort or as your first line of defense? Do you believe in Me, that I am able and

willing? When the stormy winds of life blow against you, and you don't see immediate changes, will you still declare Me faithful?"

This brings us to the third foundational truth, which is also a heading in the model prayer.

God is "our Father."

Let's focus on the first word of this heading to start: "our."

And Jesus said, "When you pray, say, 'Our Father.'" Do not personalize this because you stand the risk of thinking you're an only child. Say, "*Our* Father," because that means you have siblings, which means, ladies and gentlemen, the church of the living God is referred to as the *family* of God. That makes us all siblings. That makes us brothers and sisters. You are not alone in this effort. All of us are supposed to bear up one another. And every time we pray, "Our Father," this reminds us that everybody in our local fellowship is our sibling. I don't have the right to talk down to anyone, or to lie about anyone, or to scandalize anyone. It is terrible for me as a member of the family of God to destroy the character of my Daddy's child. When you pray, "Our Father," it is supposed to remind you of your connectivity—horizontally and vertically. You're connected to our Father, Who is above you (in a vertical relationship), and consequently, you're connected to His children, which is the same classification you hold (in a horizontal relationship).

My parents had ten children. Two passed away, and now there are eight left. I thank God today that there is no animosity, or disagreement, or family issue that I'm aware of between any of the nine siblings. This is due to how my earthly father reared us. My earthly father and mother taught us how to look out for one another. This is what we must become in the church: our brother's keeper.

Every time we pray this prayer, "Our Father," it should make us mindful of the fact that if we've done any wrong to one of our siblings in the church, we should correct that wrong with our sibling. We're siblings. We're brothers. We're sisters. We're siblings! You just found out that you had long-lost brothers and sisters! So, what does this mean? It means that if one person is celebrated, we all have a hallelujah time! If one person is mourning, we cry with that person who is mourning. We stand by them. We don't have to know them personally, but if their husband died, how are you not at the funeral? Think of your biological brother, and analyze how you would handle the situation if his wife died or if his son died. Think about how you would handle that because that's your sister-in-law or your nephew who is dead. And however you handle that in your biological family, you shouldn't be too far off with how you should handle that in the family of God.

Now let's look at the second part, our *"Father."*

When people hear the word *"Father,"* different thoughts come to mind for different people. Some people think of the person who abandoned them when they were very young, or before they were born. Some recall the abusive nature of the relationship. Others relate back to an emotionally distant provider, someone who always put food on the table but never really conveyed their love. So, based upon their personal experiences, their image of a father is not a good one. Unfortunately for these people, the temptation in this is to start with the image of fatherhood they have experienced on earth, and allow that tainted image to shape their view of our Father in heaven. So, when they hear the phrase, "our Father," even though it's accompanied by another heading, "who art in heaven," because of the image they have of fatherhood, based on their own personal experiences, negative things may come to their mind. They are more prone to view God as anything but a "good Father." Trust me when I say that you need your heavenly

Father. Statistically speaking, it has been proven that fatherless children have greater and earlier rates of sexual activity. Fatherless children are at a greater risk of drug and alcohol abuse. Fatherless children are more inclined to commit suicide. Fatherless children are usually the ones who fill the juvenile detention centers. Fatherless children are often more vulnerable to becoming victims of sexual abuse by relatives, neighbors, and friends of the resident mother. Boys who grow up without a father are more prone to confusion about their sexual identity. Fatherless children display more aggressive behavior and suffer emotional distress. Fatherless children are the most disruptive in the classroom. Fatherless children are twice as likely to drop out of high school. They are twice as likely to end up in jail, and they are four times as likely to need help for emotional and behavioral problems.

With all of this in mind, if I were the devil, I'd do everything I could to remove the father out of the home and keep him out. I'd keep him out of that house and out of the lives of the children, depriving those children of forming a proper and positive image of their father. This is a trick from hell that has become very real in our country. More single mothers are leading homes in our country than are mothers and fathers. This will not only create social problems. There is a spiritual issue here. God designed human beings so that the children should be born within the framework of a marriage, with a mother and a father, in a joint effort, raising their children. But the devil has launched an attack to get fathers out of the home, because he wants to create a negative image of fatherhood, so that these children will later have a challenge relating to "our Father."

They can't just say, "Well, these boys..." All of these statistics I have listed are scientifically proven, but they are just the offshoot to the problem. They are not the reason for the problem. The devil does not care whether you stay in school.

The devil does not mind if you stay out of jail.

What the devil is primarily concerned about is ensuring that you never really connect with God as your Father, with you as His child.

That's why the scripture says:

As many as received him, to them gave he power to become the sons of God, even to them that believed on His name.

—JOHN 1:12

The devil's target is to keep you out of a relationship with your heavenly Father because that relationship is the real key for you becoming all that you want to be. Since we know this, and we know that many may have experienced a less-than-ideal father figure in their childhood, the question becomes, what is a father supposed to look like?

The position of fatherhood is possibly one of the most important offices that any man could hope to be a part of. Far more important than any job opportunity is to be an example of God to the children of the household, and to be Jesus to the bride of the household.

For God is the Father, and Jesus treats the church as His Bride.

> *But to us there is but one God, the Father, of whom are all things, and we in him; and one Lord Jesus Christ, by whom are all things, and we by him.*
>
> — 1 CORINTHIANS 8:6

> *Husbands, love your wives, even as Christ also loved the church, and gave himself for it.*
>
> —EPHESIANS 5:25

So what is a father supposed to look like? A father provides for his family: He clothes them, he feeds them, he puts a roof over their head, and he supplies many things for the household to enjoy. A father nurtures his family: He is constantly providing loving correction where needed, strengthening the confidence and self-image of everyone in the household. A father is the protector. He protects the family members from those who would take advantage of them. He wards off financial ruin, bad relationships, and abuse in any area that might try to attack his family. The father is the head of the household. What the father says, goes. While you live in his household, there is no higher authority—not a teacher, boss, friend, or any other person on this planet who trumps the office of father to the household. If the father says to leave a relationship, tells you to quit a job, decides to move you to a different school, his word is final. So many people have problems with authority because they never had a father who taught them honor and obedience. The last thing that can truly encompass what it means to be a father is not something that people have related to fatherhood for ages, and it has cost us so much…love. To many men, being loving was the wife's job, while the husband was to be the strong, authoritative figure. This couldn't be further from the truth. God is the ultimate example of who a father is meant to be, and God defines Himself as love in the Word.

Beloved, let us love one another: for love is of God; and every one that loveth is born of God, and knoweth God. He that loveth not knoweth not God; for God is love

—1 JOHN 4:7–8

There is no greater evidence that the most important role of a father is to walk in love. And God gives us a roadmap of what that looks like, and ultimately what the father should be the example of as well as a duplicate of himself in the child.

Love endures long and is patient and kind;
love never is envious nor boils over with jealousy,
is not boastful or vainglorious,
does not display itself haughtily.

It is not conceited (arrogant and inflated with pride);

it is not rude (unmannerly) and does not act unbecomingly.

Love (God's love in us) does not insist on its own rights or its own way,

for it is not self-seeking;

it is not touchy or fretful or resentful;

it takes no account of the evil done to it [it pays no attention to a suffered wrong].

It does not rejoice at injustice and unrighteousness, but rejoices when right and truth prevail.

Love bears up under anything and everything that comes,

is ever ready to believe the best of every person,

its hopes are fadeless under all circumstances,

and it endures everything [without weakening].

*Love never fails [never fades out
or becomes obsolete or comes to
an end].*

—1 Corinthians 13:4–8a ampc

This is the roadmap of fatherhood.
This is what your heavenly Father looks
like. And here is the beautiful part about it:
whether you are a single mother who has
been struggling to keep the house together
or a child who has been abused or abandoned, you can now, in this very moment,
change your entire situation. You can let
God step into the office of Father.

*When my father and my mother
forsake me, then the Lord will
take me up.*

—Psalm 27:10

*"I will be a Father to you, and
you shall be My sons and daughters, says the Lord Almighty."*

—2 Corinthians 6:18 nkjv

Listen to God. "I will be a Father to
you." That's what He says. "I will be

a Father to you." We all have a loving Father. Your Father loves you! And He is more than enough to make up for the shortcomings of your biological father. You don't have to go through another moment in bondage because your father or spouse contaminated your view of fatherhood. God created you in His own image; He made you look like Him, and He created you to be His offspring. Since the beginning, God was all about fatherhood! He didn't just send Jesus to die on the cross to save you from eternal damnation; He sent Him so that you could be adopted into His family. He wants to be your Father, and He loves you more than you can even comprehend! He even knows the exact number of hairs that are on your head, He knit you together in the womb, and He loved you before you breathed your first breath. There is an intimacy with the Father available to us if we will choose it.

> For ye have not received the spirit of bondage again to fear; but ye have received the Spirit

of adoption, whereby we cry, Abba, Father.

—ROMANS 8:15 KJV

Abba Father is the Arabic word that in English means *"Daddy."*

We use this term when we become intimately acquainted with our Father, and in our private times of prayer, when we call Him Daddy, we begin to become aware of the true power of prayer. We are able to sense the life that we are called to be a part of. Our faith in God rises because we believe in Him, Who loves us enough to help us and do what we ask just because we, His children, asked Him to. While enjoying His presence and becoming completely vulnerable with Him, we begin enjoying the relationship that Jesus died for us to have, and then we will begin to feel and notice how a Christian is supposed to walk. God's Word will become more alive to us. The New Testament will be so rich with power and faith, and the Old Testament will reveal more of God's personality. One of the positive benefits of this is likely to be your perception of your brothers and sisters—the people all around you—will seemingly take on so much more significance in your life. Your countenance and mannerisms will begin to change and become steady. And prayer becomes something you look forward to instead of a solution to a problem in your life for you to endure. The more you walk this path, the more aware you become of God, until it gets to the point that you can't go even a few minutes without talking to God and about God. You begin to truly "know" Him and to value God, your Father, above all. When you know who He is, when you know that He is for you, that He's never against you, when you know that He loves you, and that He is the Source of *all* of your provision, then life gets exciting! God promised to keep you! He promised never to leave you! He has never, ever, ever, ever come short of His Word! That's the God you will come to know. He's a Wonderful

Counselor. He's a mighty God. He's an Everlasting Father. He's the Prince of Peace. He is a bridge when I'm crossing troubled waters. He'll be my lawyer in the courtroom. He'll be my doctor in the surgery room. He'll be my banker when my credit is found wanting. The Lord will make a way somehow. He's a Father. He's a Provider. He's a Protector. He's a Nurturer. He's a Restorer. He's our Father! He belongs to me, and He belongs to you. We are all connected to our Father because we were all saved by the same blood: the blood that gives us strength from day to day, it'll never, never lose its power! So, when you begin to pray, always start with thanksgiving, keeping in mind exactly to whom you are praying: "Our Father."

Who Art in Heaven

NOW, WHEN JESUS WAS ON EARTH, EVERY time He prayed to God, He prayed relationally. In fact, the only time we see Him in scripture talking to God and not addressing Him as "Father" was when He was dying on the cross, and He cried out, "My God! My God! Why?!" Every other time, He prayed relationally, and He called God "Father." The reason why He called Him "God" on the cross was because, in that one moment, He was covered with our sins. Consequently, He was operating outside of a relationship with His Father, so He addressed Him as "God." But when He was walking on the earth, He called God "Father." Look at what He said to the women right after the resurrection:

> *Jesus saith unto her, Touch me not; for I am not yet ascended to my Father: but go to my brethren, and say unto them, I ascend unto*

*my Father, and your Father; and
to my God, and your God.*

—JOHN 20:17 KJV

What He is saying here is that the
same help that the Father gave to Him
while He was here on earth, He would
give to us, too, because God is as much
our Father as He was Jesus' Father. And
this brings us into this current heading,
and it's where our Father resides:

"Our Father, ***who art in heaven.***"

When we speak the words, "Our
Father, who art in heaven," it suggests to
us that although He is as close to us as
a parent, God is still far above us and
beyond us. God Himself tells us as much:

*"For My thoughts are not your
thoughts, nor are your ways My
ways," says the Lord. "For as the
heavens are higher than the earth,
so are My ways higher than your
ways, and My thoughts than
your thoughts."*

—ISAIAH 55:8–9 NKJV

However, we can never be the same as Him, even though we can connect to Him. I know this seems pretty self-evident, but there is a pitfall of pride that can be found here. It's the same pitfall that Satan fell into (pun intended):

How you are fallen from heaven, O Lucifer, son of the morning! How you are cut down to the ground, you who weakened the nations! For you have said in your heart: "I will ascend into heaven, I will exalt my throne above the stars of God; I will also sit on the mount of the congregation on the farthest sides of the north; I will ascend above the heights of the clouds, I will be like the Most High." Yet you shall be brought down to Sheol, to the lowest depths of the Pit.

—ISAIAH 14:12-15 NKJV

God is above us, in a perfect position to help us! It was pride, fully manifested in Lucifer, that caused him to want to take God's place. A principle that many have come to fully understand was demonstrated here: "Pride comes before the fall." So then we should stay away from pride, and continually humble ourselves to receive the blessings of God. Humbling ourselves is not having a pity party or reminding ourselves of how imperfect we are. Humbling ourselves before the Lord has more to do with reminding ourselves of how high God is instead of how low we are!

When we meditate on how imperfect or messed up we are, we are still meditating on ourselves! Life is not all about us. So, humility then becomes less to do with our situation and more to do with God's vantage point. It becomes a position of gratitude, not for our problems, but for the solution to all of them, namely, Jesus Christ. We can funnel all of the glory to our Father, because we can see clearly that it belongs with Him. Humility is accepting the truth of our situation. Humility is reality. We were made and saved by a loving Father Who sits on the throne in heaven. We should forever be filled and overwhelmed with love and gratitude that we have the privilege and honor to connect with our Father in heaven. Reminding ourselves of His position in heaven, above us, is essential for our prayers to be heard and answered.

Now, when Jesus said, "Our Father, who art in heaven," there is also another implication that He was making. He was saying that God has a vantage point from where He can see all that is going on in our lives. So, when we say, "Our Father, who art in heaven," we are acknowledging that there is nothing going on in our lives that God does not know about. We are saying, "There's not one thing in our lives that God does not already have information about." The valley in which we may find ourselves did not catch God by surprise. Whatever will be going on one week from now, one month from now, three months from now, or next year, none of this will catch Him by surprise. We have to understand

that He's our Father, *who art in heaven!*
He has a vantage point which gives Him
a panoramic view of every facet of our
lives. He looks way beyond because of
His vantage point. Because of our limited
vision, we can only see down the road;
He can see around the corner. Sometimes
He stops some things in our lives, and
we wonder why. It's because of what's
around the corner. Sometimes we can
get so fixated on what is right in front of
us that we neglect to take into account
what God is doing behind the scenes.
God is dealing with us based on what's
ahead of us, things that we can't see yet.
He's our Father, Who art in heaven. He
has this view. He has this vantage point
that puts Him at an advantage when it
comes to our lives. So, even if something
takes us by surprise, we should catch our
emotions before they become uncontain-
able. We should rein back in all the worry,
fear, and fret that arises, then breathe a
sigh of relief, because this crisis was not
a surprise to God. It's our doubt in the
face of adversity that halts God's ability

to put His plans into action. Oh that the body of Christ would understand God's vantage point. That they would have faith in their Father Who is in heaven. That they would sing at the midnight hour in the worst sort of prison. That they would rest in the presence of hungry lions. That they would smile as He meets them in the middle of their fiery situation, and that they would rejoice as they walk to the other side of their crisis without a trace of hardship left on them—not even the smell of it!

So, when you pray, "Lord, I thank You for saving me. I thank You! I thank You! I thank You for allowing me to be Your child and for You being my Father. You are my Father, and that confirms that You are in heaven, that You are the authority in my life." When we say, "Our Father, who art in heaven," we are affirming that He is our authority. We are confirming, when we say, "Our Father, who art in heaven," that He is the source of all of our supply. We are giving Him full control of our lives. And when we say, "Our Father, who art in heaven," we are reminded of John 10, which tells us that whomever the Lord has in His hands, nobody can pluck out.

If God is your Father, and is in heaven, He can see beyond what you are looking at. On top of that, when we allow Him to be, He is in full control of the affairs of our lives!

Hallowed Be Thy Name

THE WORD *HALLOWED* SOUNDS LIKE A very spiritual word, and it might not connect with us if we are not careful. There are two truths that Jesus is trying to get across to us through this phrase, "Hallowed be Thy name." Thanksgiving and the nature of God are revealed in His name. Saying, "Hallowed be Thy name" is also saying, "Blessed be the name of God! Your name is holy, precious, of great value, and sacred." Under this heading is where you fill in everything you are thankful for—about God, about what He has done for you, in you, and through you, and about Who He is to you. Hallowing God's name is giving glory to God Himself, as well as calling attention to His name. The first truth, thanksgiving, cannot be overlooked or underestimated in any prayer. Look how often God connects prayer with thanksgiving:

Rejoice always, pray continually,
give thanks in all circumstances;
for this is God's will for you in
Christ Jesus.

— 1 THESSALONIANS 5:16–18 NIV,
emphasis mine

And whatever you do, whether in
word or deed, do it all in the name
of the Lord Jesus, **giving thanks**
to God the Father through him.

—COLOSSIANS 3:17 NIV,
emphasis mine

Be earnest and unwearied and
steadfast in your prayer life, being
both alert and intent in your
praying **with thanksgiving.**

—COLOSSIANS 4:2 AMPC,
emphasis mine

Be careful for nothing; but in every-
thing by prayer and supplication
with thanksgiving *let your requests*
be made known unto God.

—PHILIPPIANS 4:6 KJV,
emphasis mine

Thanksgiving and praise have always ushered in the presence of God. God likes to hear His children thanking Him! It sets the tone for the prayer; it forces us to meditate on the solution (God) instead of our problems. Faith is not frustrated, downtrodden, or sorrowful. Faith is full of joy and peace, and it is exciting because the future is bright with a good Father. Even the psalmist learned, before the redemption, that thanksgiving is how one should begin a prayer:

> *Enter his gates with thanksgiving and his courts with praise; give thanks to him and praise his name.*
>
> —PSALM 100:4 NIV,
> emphasis mine

Yet, we can go boldly to the throne room and thank God personally because of the redemptive work of Christ! You always have something to be thankful for. Regardless of how bleak your situation may look, thank God that you are not alone in it! Thank God that He is a good God, and a good Father, so you will refuse to let this world beat you down. When bills are piling up, symptoms are raging in your body, when you're tired, and you had some nasty things said about you, then the conditions are perfect to lift up your voice and praise God—even through the tears, through the fears, through the pain, through the sickness, through the trials, and through the suffering, because they are light and momentary, but your God is eternal. You aren't thanking Him for the problems or for making you stronger through the problems. You are thanking God that He made you, that He loves you, that He cares about you, that He knows what you have need of, that He is your Deliverer, that you have more faith in His ability to help you than in the world's ability to hurt you. When you begin to thank God in the good and the bad, you'll begin to see more good, and the bad won't affect you as much as they once did. You will begin to rest in the shadow of God Almighty. So, step one of this heading is to give thanks to your "Abba," Daddy. God's name always reveals something about His nature. It is a part of His nature that is ordained to meet your need.

As I hallow and bless and honor His name, I am simultaneously acknowledging His nature, because it is a part of His nature that will meet whatever need there is in my life.

I must know something about His name, because as I learn about His name, that helps to reveal His nature to me. And only then will I be able to recognize my need. When I hook up my need with His name, then His nature is manifested, and my need is met.

It will be hard for you to benefit from this part of the prayer if you do not understand His name. Your understanding of His nature based upon His name will help you recognize and identify how you handle your need. And when you hook up your need with His appropriate name, based on His nature, once His nature is manifested, your need will be met.

Because of this, there's no need to call God out for healing while addressing Him as *Jehovah Shalom* because the name *Jehovah Shalom* speaks about the peace of God—but you need a healing. "Oh, Lord God, our Father, I come to You recognizing You as *Jehovah Shalom.*" You need healing! So, you have to understand which part of His name deals with the nature of healing, because you're sick, and you need healing. And when you hook up your need with His name that reveals the part of His nature that ties in with your need, His nature is manifested, and your need has to be met.

The reason why so many prayers of believers have not been answered is because they lack a real understanding of His name and His nature. Their needs have been latched on to the wrong chariot. And they keep rolling, rolling, and rolling and not seeing any changes. Things are not getting better because they lack a real understanding of God's name and His nature. But when you know His name, and you understand the nature of that name, and you latch your need on to His name based on His nature, when you hallow that name, your need has to be met.

So, let's begin with *Jehovah Shalom*: the Lord my Peace. The Lord is your peace. When you know God as your peace, then the whole world could be caving in on itself and you would be smiling and praising the Lord. You could hear the worst news possible, but if you believe in *Jehovah Shalom,* then you will be unmoved by the news. Peace does not separate you from caring for others or being moved by the afflictions of others, but it does prevent others from afflicting you. You can be moved with compassion for another's situation, that is godly; Jesus was moved with compassion before many great miracles were performed. You see some people call it compassion when they feel empathy for someone else. Jesus never pitied anyone, but He did have *compassion* on them. And if someone is having a pity party, then don't you dare join them! That will mess with your peace. What you need to do is to love them and pray for them, and if you have a relationship with them, then minister to them the Word, with whatever resources you might have available. Pity feels the hopelessness of their situation, while compassion feels the pain of the situation but sees a way that situation can change. God is your peace, and if others don't receive Him as the solution to their problems, then there is not anything else you can do for them. You can love them, but don't join in with them in their pity. God is your peace! Help others join you up on the high ground of His Peace! Compare their situation to God and help them understand, as you do, that God has their back. So why worry, or be afraid? God is your peace. Hear what God says in His Word with regard to peace:

> *May the God of hope fill you with all joy and peace as you trust in him, so that you may overflow*

with hope by the power of the Holy Spirit.

—ROMANS 15:13 NIV

The LORD will give strength unto his people; the Lord will bless his people with peace.

—PSALM 29:11

You will guard him and keep him in perfect and constant peace whose mind [both its inclination and its character] is stayed on You, because he commits himself to You, leans on You, and hopes confidently in You.

—ISAIAH 26:3 AMPC

Here is the last scripture that perfectly illustrates what happens when you call upon *Jehovah Shalom*:

Do not fret or have any anxiety about anything, but in every circumstance and in everything, by prayer and petition (definite requests), with thanksgiving, continue to make your wants known to God. And God's peace [shall be yours, that tranquil state of a soul assured of its salvation through Christ, and so fearing nothing from God and being content with its earthly lot of whatever sort that is, that peace] which transcends all understanding shall garrison and mount guard over your hearts and minds in Christ Jesus.

—Philippians 4:6–7 ampc

Praise the Lord for His peace!

Now there's the name *Adonai*. This means that He's Lord of all. He's Master. He's Owner. He's Creator of everything, meaning that not only does God own everything, but there's nothing that was created without Him. That puts Him in full control of everything—including your life. When you don't have a real need and you're just giving God praise, and you're praying to Him and giving Him adoration, refer to God as *Adonai*.

"Lord, I just want to adore You. I just want to make You large in the earth realm. I just want to tell You how much I love You because You are Master, You are Owner, You are Creator, You are Sustainer, You are Deliverer. You are the Supplier! You own everything! The cattle on a thousand hills belongs to You. And I have willingly given You full rein in my life. Thank You!"

We all should have prayed an "Adonai" prayer at least two or three times a week. We should go to God as *Adonai*— even if we don't need anything. Or maybe we do, but this isn't the time when we're talking to Him about it. We're just telling Him, "Lord, You're wonderful! Lord, I come to You as Adonai. I didn't think I would make it, but You kept me, and You brought me through, and here I am. I just want to adore You! You are God, my Adonai!"

Let you and I both honor the Lord and hallow the name of Adonai! Hallowed be Adonai!

And then there's the name *El Shaddai*, Lord God Almighty, meaning that in addition to Him being omnipotent and omniscient and omnipresent, our God is all-sufficient. He never runs out of resources. And sometimes you may have a need, but you don't want to put that need before God because, as mentioned earlier, before you pray, He knows your need. So sometimes you just want to hallow the name *El Shaddai*.

> "Lord, I come before You today recognizing you as God, our Father. You are El Shaddai in my life. I know You're omnipotent. You're omnipresent. You're omniscient, but You are the all-sufficient God in my life as well. I thank You for being my Father, and I thank You for allowing me to be Your child. I hallow the name *El Shaddai!*"

You can be confident that if that name saturates and permeates the atmosphere, needs will start being met. He's the all-sufficient God! He never runs out of resources. Can you imagine being connected to the Person Who owns everything and Who never runs out of anything? Perhaps the reason why you are short so often in your life is because you never adore Him as *El Shaddai*. That's why you're coming up short. That's why there's lack. That's why you're pinching pennies. That's why you never have enough. He's waiting for you to acknowledge Him and to hallow His name, *El Shaddai*. And the best part about it is: You are the *El Shaddai*'s child, forever connected to everything that you would ever have need of! This scripture seems to perfectly capture the nature of *El Shaddai*:

> *Now to Him Who, by (in consequence of) the [action of His] power that is at work within us, is able to [carry out His purpose and] do superabundantly, far*

*over and above all that we [dare]
ask or think [infinitely beyond our
highest prayers, desires, thoughts,
hopes, or dreams].*

—EPHESIANS 3:20 AMPC

God has another name that was
revealed when He met with Moses at
the burning bush and Moses asked Him,
"Who shall I say sent me?" God said to
Moses, "Tell them 'I Am That I Am' sent
you" (Exodus 3:13–15).

"I Am that I Am" is the name that
we've come to know as "Jehovah" or
"God." God wanted to show Israel, and
by extension, God wants to assure each
of you, that He will become whatever
the need is. Lord, have mercy! That's
why, considering the way it's written
in Hebrew, Exodus 3:14 should more
accurately be translated, "I will be what
I will be." In other words, call Me. Tell
Me what you need, and I'll become that
part of My nature to meet your need. I
Am that I Am. I'll become what I need to
become. I am what I shall become when

you come. And when you come before the throne of grace, come boldly.

This name, I Am that I Am, was so holy, that the Jews wouldn't dare say the word *Jehovah* by itself. That name was so holy that they had to connect another word depicting His nature to the name Jehovah, creating a compound name so they could say it. So when you pray, you ought to take a moment to acknowledge Him and to bless Him for who He is and for what He does—because He is the great "I Am that I Am," Who loves you, protects you, guides you, looks after you, and wants to help you every day of your life. He's willing to become whatever you need Him to become.

And that's why we see *Jehovah M'kaddesh,* the Lord Who Sanctifies. That's a compound name attached to the name of *Jehovah*. Because as far as the Jews were concerned, the name *Jehovah* was too holy to just call Him that. You would have been considered disrespectful! You were being rude! Arrogant!

Presumptuous! To think, you and Jehovah are company!

We've got a problem in the body of Christ. There's no fear of God anymore. Everybody deals with God like He's their casual buddy. It's okay to be intimate with God as your Father, but never lose your holy reverence of Him. This is not just for those people who lived in Old Testament times; this is for all of us. Remember the heading "**Hallowed** be thy name"? His name is holy, and the children of Israel had the right of it.

The next name that's connected to *Jehovah,* is *Jehovah Tsidkenu* meaning, "The LORD My Righteousness." (*Righteousness* means a right standing with God.) There is nothing between you and God. You are on good terms. You can boldly be in His presence without condemnation because you are right with God. That means that wherever and whenever you stand before God in prayer, you're clothed in His righteousness! It means you do not have to come before Him as an unworthy child. The

Bible says that there's none righteous, no not one, but because you are His child and He's your Father, and because Jesus Christ shed His blood on Calvary for your sins and mine, when we go before God, He clothes us! He clothes us in His righteousness. We, in and of ourselves, are as filthy rags, none of us righteous outside of Christ. But because of Christ, we are righteous! I don't have to be a little wimp when I come to God in prayer, thinking, *who am I to qualify before this holy and righteous God?* But He says that we should come. So, we come because we've been invited to come. So don't go to Him arrogantly. Don't go to Him while you are prideful. Humble yourself. Lord, I thank You and I praise You that by the blood of Jesus, You have declared me righteous. I thank You that because of Jesus' blood on Calvary, I now have a right to come before You in prayer. And all of my brothers and sisters, even when we've shot our best shot, we would still come up short if not for Christ."

That keeps you in perspective because God has been good. And some of you all have seen tremendous successes in your life. After God has delivered, and after God has brought you through, and after God has blessed the business, and after God has allowed you to walk into your winning place, and after God made sure you were set up and you had more than enough, then remember that *all that you have* is from God! Everything that you are is because of God! Don't you dare get arrogant and pompous and full of pride because God has made a way for you. The more He blesses you, the more grateful you should be. So, I thank You and I hallow Your name, *Jehovah Tsidkenu*. See through the scriptures for yourself what it means to be righteous:

> *For no person will be justified (made righteous, acquitted, and judged acceptable) in His sight by observing the works prescribed by the Law. For [the real function of] the Law is to make men recognize and be conscious of sin [not mere*

perception, but an acquaintance with sin which works toward repentance, faith, and holy character]. But now the righteousness of God has been revealed independently and altogether apart from the Law, although actually it is attested by the Law and the Prophets, Namely, the righteousness of God which comes by believing with personal trust and confident reliance on Jesus Christ (the Messiah). [And it is meant] for all who believe. For there is no distinction, Since all have sinned and are falling short of the honor and glory which God bestows and receives. [All] are justified and made upright and in right standing with God, freely and gratuitously by His grace (His unmerited favor and mercy), through the redemption which is [provided] in Christ Jesus, Whom God put forward [before the eyes of all] as a mercy seat and propitiation by His blood *[the cleansing and life-giving sacri-fice of atonement and reconcilia-tion, to be received] through faith. This was to show God's righ-teousness, because in His divine forbearance He had passed over and ignored former sins without punishment. It was to demon-strate and prove at the present time (in the now season) that He Himself is righteous and that He justifies and accepts as righteous him who has [true] faith in Jesus. Then what becomes of [our] pride and [our] boasting? It is excluded (banished, ruled out entirely). On what principle? [On the principle] of doing good deeds? No, but on the principle of faith. For we hold that a man is justified and made upright by faith independent of and distinctly apart from good deeds (works of the Law). [The observance of the Law has nothing to do with justification.]*

—ROMANS 3:20–28 AMPC

Praise Jesus for making us righteous. If we are to boast, let us boast in Him! Amen!

The next name of God is *Jehovah Rapha,* "the Lord your Healer." And *Jehovah Rapha* is not just a Healer of bodies. He's a Healer of body, mind, and spirit. If you're sick, He'll heal your body. If you're confused, He'll heal your mind. If your spirit is broken, He'll mend your broken spirit. He's a Healer. Your healing is one of God's covenant promises. As a descendant of Abraham, healing and health are your bread. You have every right to expect to live in good health. So, when you stand before God in prayer, thank Him for being *Jehovah Rapha* while you're well. Don't wait until you're sick to acknowledge Him as *Jehovah Rapha.*

> *Lord, I thank You for being* Jehovah Rapha *in my life. That's why I'm well! God is a Healer! God is a Restorer! God is a Keeper of Body, Mind and Spirit!*

Hear from His Word about God, your Healer:

"If you diligently heed the voice of the LORD *your God and do what is right in His sight, give ear to His commandments and keep all His statutes, I will put none of the diseases on you which I have brought on the Egyptians. **For I am the** LORD **who heals you.**"*

—EXODUS 15:26 NKJV,
emphasis mine

Beloved, I pray that you may prosper in all things and be in health, just as your soul prospers.

—3 JOHN 1:2 NKJV

Surely He has borne our griefs and carried our sorrows; yet we esteemed Him stricken, smitten by God, and afflicted. But He was wounded for our transgressions, He was bruised for our iniquities; The chastisement for our peace

was upon Him, and by His stripes
we are healed.

—Isaiah 53:4–5 NKJV

O Lord *my God, I cried out to*
You, and You healed me.

—Psalm 30:2 NKJV

Then they cried out to the Lord *in*
their trouble, and He saved them
out of their distresses. He sent His
word and healed them, and deliv-
ered them from their destructions.
Oh, that men would give thanks
to the Lord *for His goodness, and*
for His wonderful works to the
children of men!

—Psalm 107:19–21 NKJV

He heals the brokenhearted and
binds up their wounds.

—Psalm 147:3 NKJV

Now there is one last verse I want to
share with you before we consider the
next name of God:

*Heal me, O L*ORD*, and I shall be healed; save me, and I shall be saved, for You are my praise.*

—JEREMIAH 17:14 NKJV

When the Lord heals you, the Lord becomes your Healer. When His *Raphe* nature comes on the scene, there is no sickness on earth or in hell that can override the healing power of *Jehovah Raphe* in your body. "Heal me, and I shall be healed."

The next name is a powerful one: *Jehovah Rohi,* "the Lord your Shepherd." Now here's another key in scripture and a key for your prayer life: one of the best ways to pray is to pray back the scriptures to God. So, as you pray and thank God for being your Father and for making you His child, for living in heaven and for ruling over your life, then say to Him, "Lord, I hallow Your name as *Jehovah Rohi.* I bless Your name, I thank You that You are my Shepherd. Good God, help me get through this." As you do that, that's a good time for you to then pray back the Twenty-Third Psalm to Him. Don't just recite it, but say it from your heart; make it your own! Like this:

"Lord, our Father, who is in heaven, I thank You for being my Shepherd. And because You are my Shepherd, I shall not want for anything. And since You are my Shepherd, You make me to lie down in green pastures. You lead me. You order my footsteps and put me right beside still waters. Although my soul has been restless because of some errors in my life, You restore my soul. And even though I walk through the valley of the shadow of death, because You're my Shepherd, I won't worry. I'll fear no evil because You're my Shepherd. And because You're my Shepherd, I know You are with me. You have a rod in one hand and a staff in the other hand, and they comfort me. And at the appropriate time, Lord, You anoint my head with oil.

And You don't just give me a few drops here and a few drops there. You bless me until my cup runs over! Whenever there is trouble in my life, You don't leave me alone. You don't want me to be distracted. So, you have assigned goodness and mercy to follow me. I bless You as *Jehovah Rohi* because You are my Shepherd."

Sometimes when you come to pray, you may come to God and you don't know what to do or say because your life is so screwed up. This doesn't mean you're sinful. There's just a lot of mess going on around you. Sometimes when you come to pray, you may not know which direction to take. But because *Jehovah Rohi* is your Shepherd, He will go in front of you. And He'll clear down the obstacles and the hindrances. He'll remove all of the junk in your way to give you a clear path. If you are doubting what to do, when to do it, how to do it, or where to do it, then call upon your *Jehovah Rohi* for guidance, for He is your Shepherd! Jesus gives us some keen insight on this in John 10:

> *"Most assuredly, I say to you, he who does not enter the sheepfold by the door, but climbs up some other way, the same is a thief and a robber. But he who enters by the door is the shepherd of the sheep. To him the doorkeeper opens, and the sheep hear his voice; and he calls his own sheep by name and leads them out. And when he brings out his own sheep, he goes before them; and the sheep follow him, for they know his voice. Yet they will by no means follow a stranger, but will flee from him, for they do not know the voice of strangers." Jesus used this illustration, but they did not understand the things which He spoke to them. Then Jesus said to them again, "Most assuredly, I say to you, I am the door of the sheep. All who ever came before Me are thieves and robbers, but the sheep*

did not hear them. I am the door. If anyone enters by Me, he will be saved, and will go in and out and find pasture. The thief does not come except to steal, and to kill, and to destroy. I have come that they may have life, and that they may have it more abundantly. I am the good shepherd. The good shepherd gives His life for the sheep. But a hireling, he who is not the shepherd, one who does not own the sheep, sees the wolf coming and leaves the sheep and flees; and the wolf catches the sheep and scatters them. The hireling flees because he is a hireling and does not care about the sheep. I am the good shepherd; and I know My sheep, and am known by My own. As the Father knows Me, even so I know the Father; and I lay down My life for the sheep. And other sheep I have which are not of this fold; them also I must bring, and they will hear My voice; and there will be one flock and one shepherd."

—JOHN 10:1–16 NKJV

He will feed His flock like a shepherd; He will gather the lambs with His arm, and carry them in His bosom, and gently lead those who are with young.

—ISAIAH 40:11 NKJV

You see, it is not ultimately the name in and of itself that is going to bring the manifestation of the answers you are looking for in life. It is belief in the name, and in the nature that it represents. It is feeding on His Word, meditating upon what it says, and acting on it that will build up your faith in God's name in whatever area you have a need. Remember, it's not formula-praying to an indifferent God. It is prayer to our Father in heaven. It's about giving thanks to God and blessing His name. And before you present anything that you need or want to Him, you first must recognize and believe in who God is. That is the power behind the names of God! God is always the Healer whether you believe it or not. But He cannot become your Healer until you believe that He is. So, search the Scriptures. Spend time meditating on Who God said He is. And the next time you begin to pray, follow these first few headings, and speak to your Daddy with thanksgiving and full assurance of who He is.

About The Author

Bishop Neil C. Ellis is the presiding prelate of the Global United Fellowship (GUF), with more than 1,400 churches in 42 countries. GUF serves as an international body of spiritual leaders, fellowships, and congregations united to strategically plan, implement, and execute transformative and generational change.

Bishop Ellis is the senior pastor of Mount Tabor Church in Nassau, Bahamas. This church has grown from 11 charter members in 1987 to thousands of members and thousands more who are a part of the Internet Church, Mount Tabor Anytime. As a pastor to pastors, he mentors a large number of pastors around The Bahamas, Europe, and the United States and serves as a counselor and advisor to hundreds of pastors around the world.

Bishop Ellis has been recognized by Her Majesty, Queen Elizabeth of England for rendering distinguished services in Commonwealth nations and is also the recipient of the 2010 Trumpet Award for Spiritual Enlightenment. He is the youngest living inductee in the International Civil Rights Walk of Fame located in Atlanta, Georgia. He is also the author of several books and is a much sought after conference speaker and prophetic teacher.

Bishop Ellis and his wife reside in Nassau, Bahamas along with their two children.